BIG MACHINES

D0996289

Tractors

David and Penny Glover

W

FRANKLIN WATTS
LONDON • SYDNEY

First published in 2004 by Franklin Watts
96 Leonard Street, London EC2A 4XD

Franklin Watts Australia
45-51 Huntley Street
Alexandria, NSW 2015

Series editor: Sarah Peutrill
Designer: Richard Langford
Art director: Jonathan Hair
Reading consultant: Margaret Perkins, Institute of Education, University of Reading

Picture credits:
Geoff Ashcroft: 4, 20, 23t. Nigel Cattlin/Holt Studios: 15b, 21t. Courtesy of John Deere
Ltd: front cover, 6, 7, 8, 9t, 10, 11b, 12, 13, 14, 15t, 16, 17b, 18, 19t, 23b. Willem Harinck/Holt
Studios: 22. Rosie Jordan/Holt Studios: 19b. Inga Spence/Holt Studios: 21b.

With particular thanks to John Deere Ltd for permission to use their photos.

A CIP catalogue record for this book is available from the British Library.

ISBN 0 7496 5563 1

Printed in Malaysia

Contents

Tractor work

Tractors are big machines. They can do lots of different kinds of work. They move soil on building sites, drag logs in forests, and tow trailers on the road.

BIG FACT

There are more than ten million tractors at work in the world!

This tractor is pulling a trailer.

Tractors can lift, as well as pull or push.

Tractors are mainly used on farms. Farmers use them to pull ploughs and to work other farm machines. Tractors can pull heavy loads over rough ground.

Big wheels

Tractors must cross all kinds of ground. Farmers drive them along muddy tracks, over bumpy fields and even through shallow water.

The tractor's big wheels let it cross sticky mud and rough rocks. Small wheels would sink or get stuck.

Huge tyres spread the tractor's weight. They flatten bumps and stop the tractor sinking on soft ground.

Groove

Axle

Tyre

The axle is the rod on which the wheel is fixed.

Deep grooves help the tyres grip in soft soil. They work like the grips on the bottom of trainers.

The engine

A tractor has a very strong engine to give it the power to move and pull loads.

The engine is at the front of the tractor. ▶

Engine

BIG FACT

A big tractor engine has the power of 200 horses!

The engine runs on diesel fuel. The fuel burns inside the engine, making a hot gas that pushes the parts around.

The engine turns gears in the gearbox. These are connected to the driveshaft, which turns the tractor's wheels.

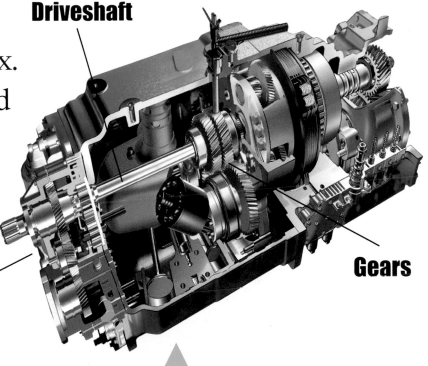

Driveshaft

Gears

Gearbox

Gears are wheels with teeth. They carry the force from the engine through the driveshaft to the big back wheels, just like the gears on a bicycle.

The different machines the tractor pulls, such as a plough, sometimes need power too. They get this from the tractor's engine.

Driveshaft

A driveshaft turns a grass cutter. ▶

Driving seat

The tractor driver sits on a seat inside the cab. The cab is very strong. It must keep the driver safe if the tractor accidentally topples over in a ditch or on a steep slope.

The cab is high above the ground so the driver has a good view.

Control panel

Steering wheel

The seat is soft and comfortable. The farmer sometimes has to sit in the tractor all day.

Seat

The driver steers the tractor with the steering wheel. The steering wheel turns the front wheels to the right or left to make the tractor turn. Levers, switches and buttons work all the tractor parts.

Pulling

A tractor's main job is pulling. That's how it got its name. The word 'traction' means pulling power.

The farmer hitches a plough to the back of the tractor. This means the tractor can pull the plough across the field. Ploughing breaks up the soil. The tractor's big wheels stop it skidding as the blades cut into the soil.

BIG FACT

A modern plough can have 12 blades!

Plough

The curved plough blades are called shares. Their special shape turns the soil over, making lines called furrows across the field.

The tractor can lift the blades when all the ploughing is done.

Blades (Shares)

Tractor to the rescue! When another vehicle is stuck in the mud, a tractor can pull it free.

Lifting and loading

When hay needs stacking, a tractor can do the job. A lifting arm is fitted at the front of the tractor. The farmer drives the tractor forwards to pick up the load. Then the farmer moves a lever to lift it into the air.

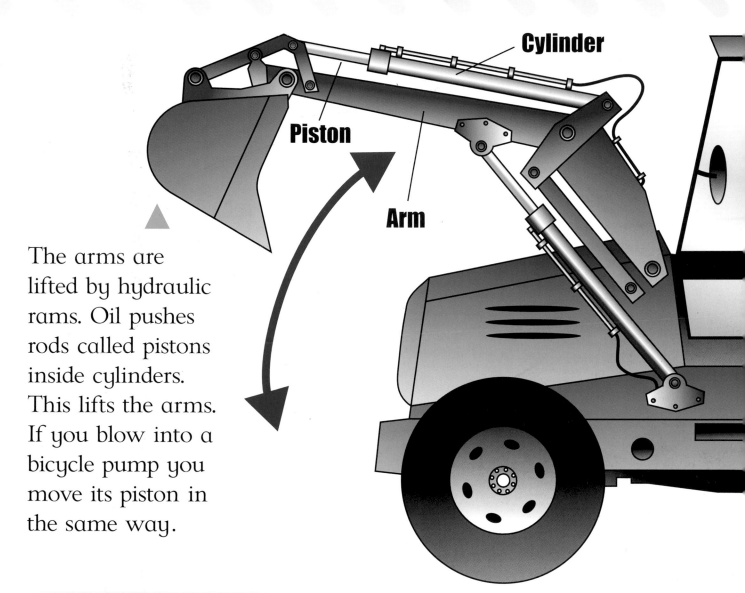

Cylinder

Piston

Arm

The arms are lifted by hydraulic rams. Oil pushes rods called pistons inside cylinders. This lifts the arms. If you blow into a bicycle pump you move its piston in the same way.

A tractor can also be fitted with a scoop to lift sand or soil.

Sound and light

A tractor has all the lights a car has - headlights, rear lights, brake lights and flashing indicators. This means it can travel on the road at any time.

Indicator lights

Spotlights

Head lamps

When the crops are ready, there is no time to lose. Tractors are fitted with extra spotlights so the farmer can gather the harvest through the night.

CD player   **Two- way radio**

The driver can keep in touch with other workers on the farm with the two-way radio.

◄ Music from a CD player keeps this driver entertained as he works alone in the fields.

On the road

At harvest time there are lots of tractors with trailers on the roads. The trailers carry vegetables, fruit or grain. The farmer takes each load to a barn where it is stored, waiting to be taken to a supermarket or a food factory.

Trailer

A hydraulic
ram tilts the
trailer.

**Hydraulic
ram**

Load

A back gate
is opened,
and the load
pours out.

Enormous tractors

A big tractor can plough faster than a small one. It can pull several machines in 'gangs' to plough and level more soil at the same time.

Big tractors are four-wheel-drive. This means the engine turns the front wheels as well as the back wheels.

▲ Four-wheel-drive and more wheels gives the tractor better grip.

A big tractor has twice as many wheels to spread its great weight over the soft ground.

BIG FACT

In tractor-pulling contests special tractors with huge engines compete to pull the biggest load!

This tractor has eight wheels.

Make it yourself

Make a box model tractor and trailer.

You will need:

An adult to help

Paints

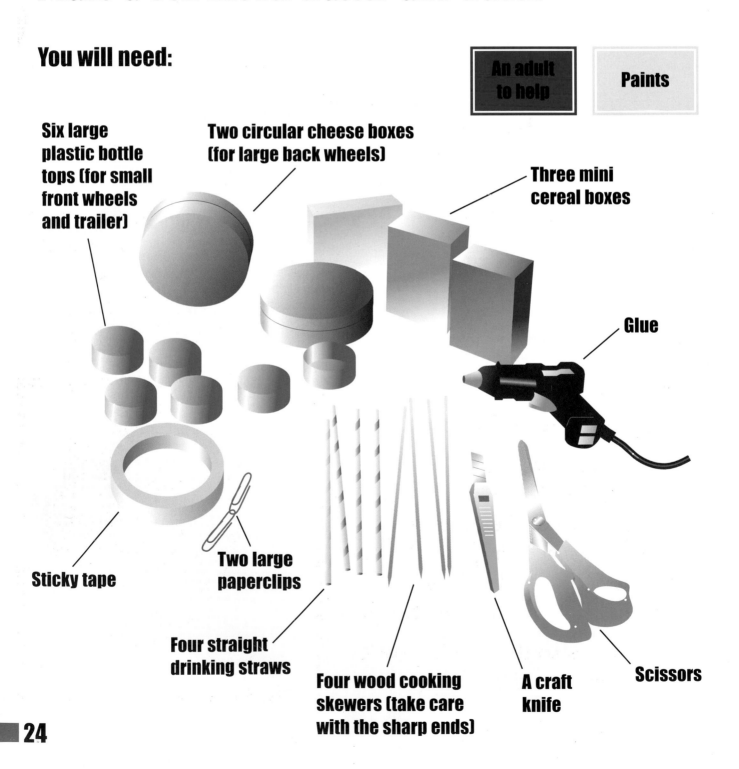

Six large plastic bottle tops (for small front wheels and trailer)

Two circular cheese boxes (for large back wheels)

Three mini cereal boxes

Glue

Sticky tape

Two large paperclips

Four straight drinking straws

Four wood cooking skewers (take care with the sharp ends)

A craft knife

Scissors

SAFETY! An adult must help you with the cutting and sticking.

1. Glue two boxes together to make the tractor body and cab.

1.

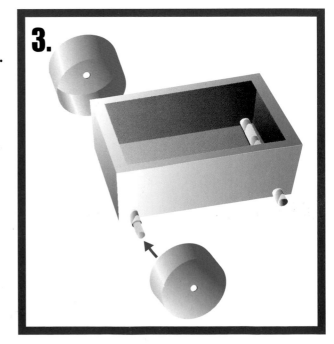

2.

This straw is a bit higher for the larger back wheel.

2. Cut the side from one of the cereal boxes to make the trailer body.

Mark and make pairs of holes in the tractor and trailer bodies. Push a straw through each pair of holes. Cut to length.

3. Slide the wooden skewers through the straws. These are axles.

Make small holes in the centres of the wheels. Push the large wheels onto the axles at the back of the tractor. Glue them in place. Do the same with the small wheels at the front of the tractor and the trailer.

Cut the axles so they do not stick out too far from the wheels.

3.

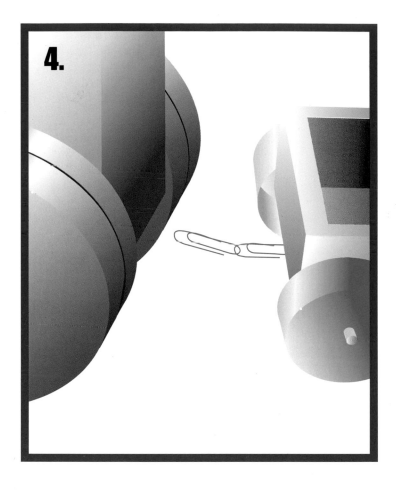

4. Tape or glue one paperclip to the back of the tractor and one to the front of the trailer. This is the hitch.

5. Decorate your model with paint.

Hitch your trailer to your tractor (clip the paperclips together). Test your model on a rough surface. Which roll best, the big tractor wheels or the small ones?

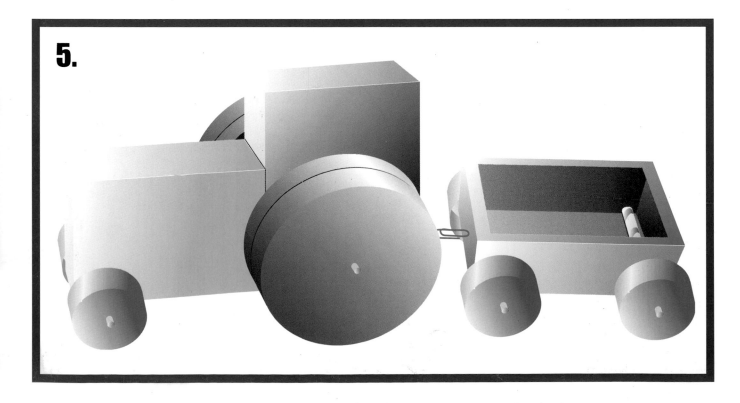

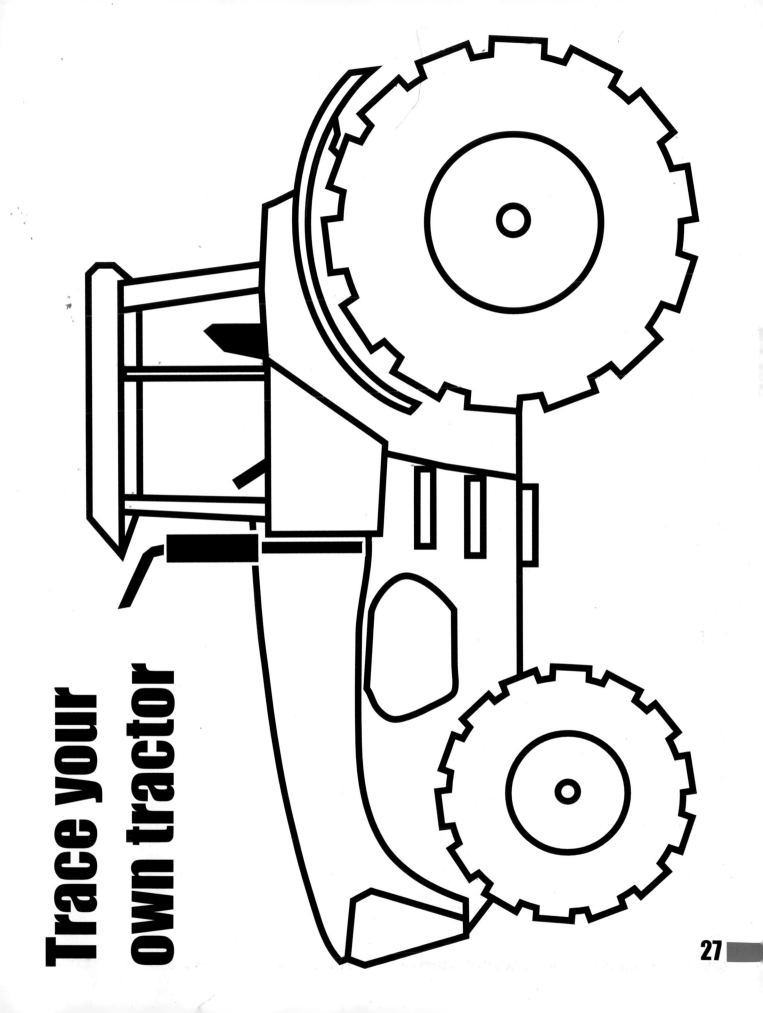

Trace your own tractor

Tractor words

axle
The rod through the centre of a wheel.

cab
The part of a tractor in which the driver sits.

diesel
The fuel a tractor engine uses to make it go.

engine
The part of a machine that burns fuel to make the forces that turn its wheels and move its parts.

four-wheel-drive
A tractor, or another vehicle, in which the engine turns all four wheels.

gear
A wheel with teeth that carries the turning force from the engine to other parts of a machine.

groove
A deep line cut into a wheel.

hydraulic ram

The part on a tractor machine that pushes to lift a load, or tip a trailer. The ram is worked by oil, which pushes a rod called a piston along a cylinder.

load

The things the tractor carries in its trailer, such as vegetables, fruit or grain.

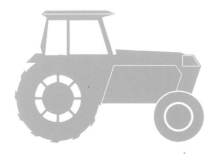

plough

A farm machine that breaks up the soil in a field when it is pulled behind a tractor.

spotlight

A very bright light that lights up the area at which it is pointed.

trailer

A wagon or truck pulled by a tractor to carry a load.

tyre

The rubber ring filled with air on the outside of a wheel.

Index